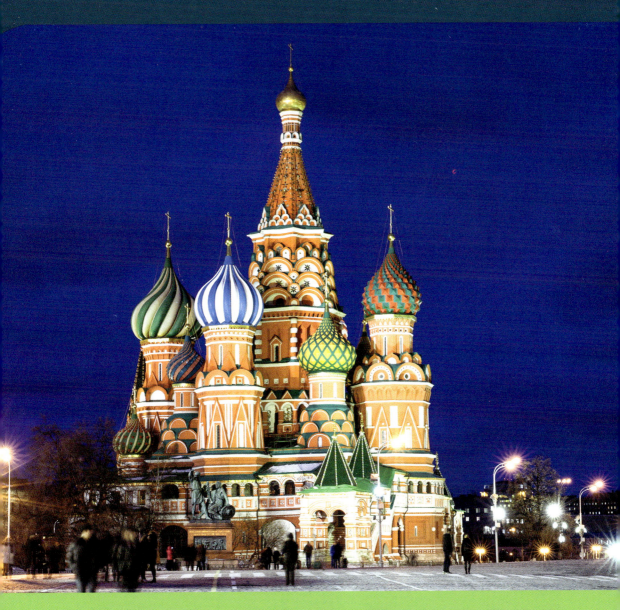

EXPLORE RUSSIA
12 KEY FACTS

by Alicia Klepeis

www.12StoryLibrary.com

12-Story Library is an imprint of Bookstaves.

Photographs ©: ErmakovaElena/iStockphoto, cover, 1; Nadezhda Bolotina/Shutterstock. com, 4; Luxerendering/Shutterstock.com, 5; Gregory A. Pozhvanov/Shutterstock.com, 6; Andrei Gilbert/Shutterstock.com, 7; Sergey Chayko/Shutterstock.com, 8; Frederic Legrand - COMEO/Shutterstock.com, 10; Pukhov K/Shutterstock.com, 11; kemdim/Shuttterstock. com, 12; Sorbis/Shutterstock.com, 13; fotosparrow/Shutterstock.com, 14; Dmitry A. Mottl/ CC3.0, 15; Everett Historical/Shutterstock.com, 16; Anton Gvozdikov/Shutterstock.com, 17; akedesign/Shutterstock.com, 18; konstantinks/Shutterstock.com, 19; Pavel L Photo and Video/Shutterstock.com, 20; Internet Archive Book Images, 21; A_Lesik/Shutterstock.com, 22; freeskyline/Shutterstock.com, 23; De Visu/Shutterstock.com, 24; Witolda/Shutterstock. com, 25; BestPhotoPlus/Shutterstock.com, 26; demamiel62/Shutterstock.com, 27; Globe Turner/Shutterstock.com, 28; Nannucci/iStockphoto, 29

ISBN
978-1-63235-560-7 (hardcover)
978-1-63235-615-4 (paperback)
978-1-63235-677-2 (ebook)

Library of Congress Control Number: 2018940814

Printed in the United States of America
Mankato, MN
June 2018

About the Cover

St. Basil's Cathedral, located in Red Square in Moscow, was completed in 1560. It is now a museum.

Access free, up-to-date content on this topic plus a full digital version of this book. Scan the QR code on page 31 or use your school's login at 12StoryLibrary.com.

Table of Contents

1

Russia Is the Biggest Country in the World

Russia is the world's largest country. It covers about one-tenth of all land on Earth.

It is more than 6.6 million square miles (17.1 million sq km) in size. And almost twice the size of the United States.

Russia is so big it spans two continents. The western part is in Europe. The eastern part lies in Asia. The Ural Mountains form the border between Europe and Asia.

Russia has coasts on three of the world's major oceans. The Atlantic is to the west. The Arctic Ocean is to the north. The Pacific is to the east. It shares borders with 14 countries. These include China, Mongolia, Norway and Finland.

The Ural Mountains run north to south through western Russia.

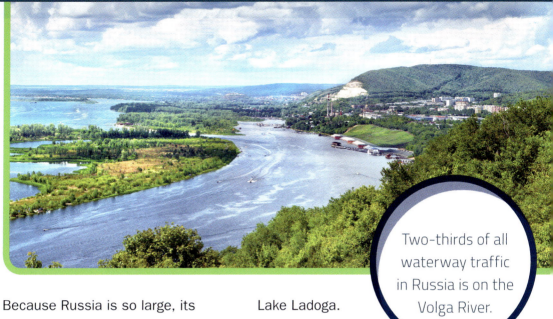

Because Russia is so large, its landscape is varied. It has deserts, icy coastlines, and tall mountains. Mt. Elbrus in the south is the highest peak. It reaches 18,510 feet (5,642 m) into the air. Russia's giant lakes include Lake Baikal and Lake Ladoga. Russia has around 100,000 rivers. Much of the land consists of vast treeless plains called steppes.

11
Time zones in Russia.

- Russia is the world's largest country.
- Russia stretches across Europe and Asia.
- The landscape includes mountains, deserts, and lakes.
- Plains cover a large amount of Russia.

THE VOLGA RIVER

The Volga is Russia's most important river. It's the longest river in Europe. The Volga begins northwest of Moscow. It flows for about 2,300 miles (3,700 km) to the Caspian Sea. Most of Russia's people live within the Volga region. The river is used for transportation. It is a source of irrigation. It also provides hydroelectric power.

Winters Are Long and Summers Are Short

Because Russia is so huge, the climate varies from place to place. In most of Russia, winters are long and summers are short. Spring and fall are brief. The average winter temperature is 14 degrees Fahrenheit (-10°C). Summers in Moscow can get as hot as 99 degrees Fahrenheit (37°C). The coast along the Black Sea has a subtropical climate. The city of Sochi has warm, comfortable temperatures with much rainfall.

Siberia is a vast region in northern Russia. It is colder during the winter than any other inhabited place on Earth. Oymyakon is a remote village in Siberia. In January 2018, the local thermometer broke after recording a temperature of -80 degrees Fahrenheit (-62°C).

Russia has three main biomes. They are steppe, taiga, and tundra. Each has its own plants and animals. The steppe is dry grassland. Many coniferous trees grow in the taiga. The tundra is mostly barren. Mosses and lichens grow there. Reindeer and musk oxen make their homes in the tundra.

Some animals are unique to Russia. One is the Baikal seal, found in Lake Baikal. It's the only seal in the world that lives exclusively in fresh water. Russia is also home to many endangered species. These include the European mink and the beluga whale.

Average annual precipitation on the steppes is 10–18 inches (26–46 cm).

540
Estimated number of Amur tigers left in the world.

- Northern Russia is very cold.
- Russia's three main biomes are steppe, taiga, and tundra.
- Russia is home to a wide variety of animals.

THINK ABOUT IT

In 1917, Czar Nicholas II created Russia's first *zapovednik*, or nature reserve. He set aside land near Lake Baikal in Siberia. Do you think it is important for countries to protect certain natural areas? Why or why not?

Over 100,000 seals live in Baikal Lake.

Russia Has a Complicated History

As an independent nation, Russia is very young. It is not even 30 years old. But people have lived there for millennia. Permanent human settlements date back to the sixth century. Early people came south from Scandinavia. They mixed with Slavic people and built the city of Kiev. It ruled over most of European Russia for hundreds of years. Eventually, this area became Belarus, Ukraine, and Muscovy. Moscow was the capital of Muscovy.

Mongol invaders took over during the thirteenth century. In 1480, the Muscovites drove them out. A leader named Ivan the Terrible unified the region. Russia grew in power. Its territory expanded eastward.

In 1682, Peter the Great became czar. He was just 10 years old. For over 40 years, he worked to modernize Russia. But the czarist system wasn't great for all Russians. Some were very rich. Others lived in poverty.

Erected in the city of Oryol in 2016, the first-ever monument to Ivan the Terrible caused controversy.

8

A revolution took place in 1917. The czar was overthrown. A few months later, a communist group took over. Vladimir Lenin, the group's leader, created a new nation. It was the Union of Soviet Socialist Republics (USSR). It was called the Soviet Union for short.

The USSR and the United States were allies during World War II. But that changed after the war. Tensions ran high. This period was known as the Cold War. Nearly 50 years later, the USSR split up.

1991
Year when Russia became independent of the USSR.

- Kiev was an important city for many centuries.
- Russia was ruled by czars before communists took control.
- The Cold War followed World War II.

TIMELINE

Approximately 500 CE: First permanent settlement in Russia.

Ninth century: Kiev is founded.

1237–40: The Mongol invasion.

1547–84: Ivan the Terrible reigns as the first czar.

1682–1725: Peter the Great rules.

1917: The Russian Revolution takes place.

1922: The USSR is founded.

1991: The USSR breaks up and Russia becomes an independent country.

The Government Is a Federation

Russia is divided into 83 administrative units. Each unit is responsible for certain things. But all the units are controlled by the central government. It is based in Moscow.

The president of Russia is the head of state. Vladimir Putin was president from 2000 to 2008. He was elected president again in 2012 and 2018.

The prime minister is the head of the government. This person is appointed by the president. Dmitry Medvedev was made prime minister in 2012.

Russia's legislature is called the Federal Assembly. It is made up of two houses. The upper house is the Federation Council, with 170 members. The lower house is the State Duma, with 450 members. The two houses work together to make laws.

The constitution is the law of the land across Russia. The Constitutional Court interprets the constitution. It decides how the country's laws are applied. Other courts include the Supreme Court.

Russia's military has several branches. These include Ground Troops, Airborne Troops, Aerospace

Vladimir Putin won 76 percent of the vote in 2018.

Russia has the second-most powerful military in the world, after the United States.

Forces, and the Navy. Over one million Russians are active members. Males between 18 and 27 must serve for one year in the military.

61

Women in the Russian State Duma between 2012 and 2018.

- Russia has a president and a prime minister.
- There are 83 administrative units in Russia's government.
- Russian males between the ages of 18 and 27 must perform one year of military service.

RUSSIA UNDER PUTIN: DEMOCRACY OR DICTATORSHIP?

Vladimir Putin first took office in 2000. Since then, many people have been concerned about how Russia's government is being run. There have been reports of corruption in all branches of government. People have complained of interference with free and fair political elections. At times, Russia has limited free speech and the right of the people to assemble.

5

Russia Has a Wealth of Natural Resources

Russia is the world's third-largest exporter of coal.

Russia has the seventh-largest economy in the world. Its gross domestic product (GDP) is $4 trillion. That figure represents the value of all the goods Russia produces in a year.

Russia has a wide variety of natural resources. It has rich deposits of coal, oil, and natural gas. The Ural Mountains contain many valuable minerals, gems, and ores. Gold, platinum, nickel, and copper are mined there. Vast forests grow in Siberia and the Russian Far East. The timber is used to make wood and paper.

Nearly two out of three Russian workers have service jobs. Some work in schools or hospitals. Others have jobs in stores, museums, banks, or hotels. Almost 28 percent of Russians have industrial jobs. Russia produces aircraft and ships, agricultural machinery and communications equipment.

Fewer than one out of ten Russians work in agriculture. Some of Russia's most important crops are grains like barley and oats. But the nation also produces sugar beets, sunflower seeds, beef, and milk.

Russia exports large amounts of petroleum, coal, and aluminum. But the country doesn't make everything it needs. So it imports goods from other countries. Imports include vehicles, machinery, and medicine. Russia's most important trading partners include China, Germany, the United States, and the Netherlands.

13

Percent of Russia's land used for agriculture.

- Russia has one of the world's largest economies.
- Processing coal, oil, and timber contributes to the economy.
- Most Russian workers have service jobs.
- Russia trades its goods with many countries.

Many Russians work in the service industry.

Education Is Important to Russians

Children in Russia are required to go to school for 11 years. They start primary school at age six. They study science, math, physical education, the arts, and technology.

After their first nine years of general education, students have a choice. They can continue with a general education. Or they can take vocational education courses. These students might train to be hairdressers or auto mechanics.

The Russian government provides free education to all students through high school. Those who score high on a state exam can attend university for free. The government will pay for it. Other students can choose to pay for their higher education.

Russian universities offer many different fields of study. Medicine, engineering, and business are among the most popular. More than half of all Russian adults have a degree. As a result, Russia is one of the most educated countries in the world.

Lomonosov Moscow State University has over 6,000 professors.

Russians have celebrated Knowledge Day since 1984.

There are nearly one thousand universities in Russia. About 5.2 million students attended in 2014–15. The country's oldest university is Lomonosov Moscow State University. It was established in 1755. This university often ranks among the world's best in 20 subjects including math and physics.

34

Weeks per year Russian children go to school.

- Russian children must attend 11 years of schooling.
- After nine years of schooling, students choose between general education and vocational training.
- Some students receive a free university education.

KNOWLEDGE DAY

September 1 is a special day of the year for Russian students. Known as Knowledge Day, it's the first day of a new school year. Children bring bouquets of flowers to their teachers. Sometimes the head teachers or administrators of schools give inspiring speeches to their pupils. Classes don't begin until the following day.

Russia Is Strong in Science and Technology

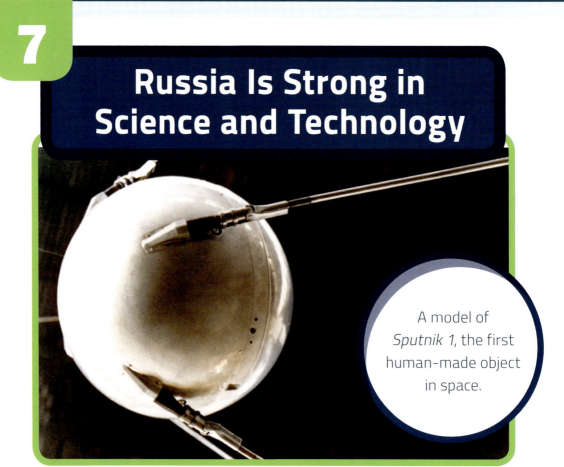

A model of *Sputnik 1*, the first human-made object in space.

Russia is a world leader in science and technology. The nation has a long history of scientific achievements. Fifteen Russians have won Nobel Prizes in scientific areas. Twelve were in physics.

Science and technology boomed when Russia was part of the USSR. There was a strong focus on nuclear physics during this time. The Soviet Union was the second country to develop the atomic bomb.

The Soviet Union once had a highly successful space program. In 1957, it launched the world's first artificial satellite, *Sputnik 1*, into space. In 1961, Soviet cosmonaut Yuri Gagarin was the first human to go into space.

Russia continues to make progress in science and technology. The government is developing national

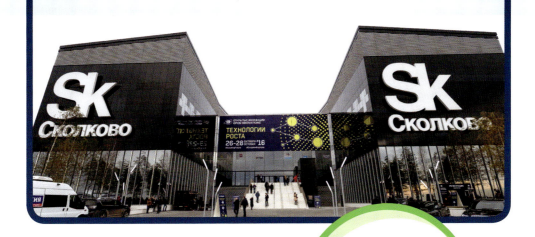

research and high-tech centers. An example is the technopark in Skolkovo outside of Moscow. It was modeled after Silicon Valley in the United States.

Russia's technology industry is growing. One field of growth is nanotechnology. This involves building very tiny things, such as computer chips. Another important area is computer software design.

7,000 people work at the Skolkovo Technopark.

20
Approximate number of dogs sent into space by the Soviet Union.

- Russians have earned many Nobel prizes in science.
- The Soviet Union launched the world's first artificial satellite and the first human into space.
- New research and high-tech centers are booming in Russia.

THINK ABOUT IT

The USSR was a pioneer in space exploration. The 1950s and '60s saw a space race between the Soviet Union and the United States. But Russia's space program has been much less active in recent decades. Try to find out why by doing research online.

Russia Has Large Transportation and Communication Networks

The Moscow Metro is the world's busiest subway.

1,218
Airports in Russia.

- Russia has large road and railway networks for the transport of people and goods.
- Cell phone and internet use in Russia have boomed over the last two decades.
- Many Russians get their news from TV.

Staying connected in a huge country is a big challenge. Russia has nearly 800,000 miles (1.3 million km) of roads. That's the fifth-largest road network in the world. Some cities have serious traffic problems. Moscow and Kansk are two examples.

In many Russian cities, people use public transportation. The subway is an easy and popular way to get around. Several of Moscow's subway stations are cultural heritage sites. They have mosaics and statues.

Railways link cities and towns across Russia. The Trans-Siberian railway connects Moscow to Vladivostok. This journey of 6,152 miles (9,258 km) takes about a week. Airplanes carry people and cargo throughout the country and internationally.

Cell phone use in Russia has skyrocketed. In 1998, there were fewer than one million cell phone subscribers. By 2016, there were 255 million.

Millions of Russians communicate over the internet. Moscow was the first city in Europe to offer Wi-Fi on trains. The Wi-Fi works not just in stations but during the journey.

Most Russians get their news from television. The government controls some stations. But more Russians are choosing to pay for satellite TV. It offers variety and more channels to watch.

RIVERBOAT TRAVEL IN RUSSIA

Locals and tourists alike enjoy traveling by water in Russia. With thousands of rivers, riverboat cruises are popular. A favorite route connects Moscow with St. Petersburg. These cities are just 400 miles (650 km) apart. Yet a cruise between them includes travel on 10 different rivers. River travel gives people a closer look at the landscape and lives of Russian villagers.

A hydrofoil boat on the Neva River in St. Petersburg.

Many Ethnic Groups Call Russia Home

More than 142 million people live in Russia. But the country's population is declining. More people today choose to have smaller families. Others decide not to have children at all.

Almost 78 percent of Russia's people belong to the Russian ethnic group. In addition, there are more than 120 different ethnic groups. The Tatars, Ukrainians, and Bashkir are a few examples. Often these groups have their own languages and traditions.

Russian is the official language. Approximately 80 percent of the people speak Russian as their first and only language.

A Russian family in Moscow.

196,000

Foreign workers who came to Russia in 2016 and stayed.

- Russia has many ethnic groups.
- Most people speak the Russian language.
- Many different languages are used by a small portion of the population.
- Many Russians do not practice any religion.

THE CHUKCHI

The Chukchi are indigenous people of Siberia. They live in a large area. It stretches from the Bering Strait to Siberia's Kolyma River valley. They also dwell along the Pacific and Arctic coasts of northeast Asia. In the past, the Chukchi who lived along the coasts fished and hunted Arctic sea animals. The Reindeer Chukchi made their living raising herds of reindeer. Today many Chukchi have service jobs. Their traditional way of life is disappearing.

Schools teach English and German. More than 100 minority languages are also spoken in Russia today.

An indigenous Chukchi man in 1824.

Between 10 and 15 percent of Russians follow the Russian Orthodox religion. Another 10 to 15 percent are Muslim. Many Russians don't practice any religion at all. The Soviet government was officially atheist. For decades, it tried to wipe out religion. Believers were persecuted and places of worship were destroyed.

21

10

Russia Has a Rich Culture

The Bolshoi Ballet has performed at the Bolshoi Theatre in Moscow since 1825.

Kandinsky is known for his bright, colorful paintings.

Russia's classical composers have produced some amazing music. Pyotr Ilyich Tchaikovsky wrote many famous pieces. The ballets *Swan Lake* and *The Nutcracker* are two examples. An incredible ballet tradition exists in Russia. Both the Bolshoi and Mariinsky ballet companies are internationally known.

Art, music, theater, and dance are all important parts of Russian culture. Russia has many world-class art museums. One is the State Hermitage Museum in St. Petersburg. Russian artist Vasily

Russians enjoy many different holidays. June 12 is the Day of Russia. This day marks Russia's independence from the Soviet Union in 1991. People celebrate across the country with fireworks displays. Some Russian holidays are Christian

SPORTS IN RUSSIA

Russians of all ages enjoy sports. Ice hockey is very popular. So is basketball. Lots of Russians enjoy playing and watching soccer as well. In 2018, Russia hosted the FIFA World Cup. Russian gymnasts and figure skaters have brought home many Olympic medals. Tennis player Maria Sharapova has won numerous tournaments. These include Wimbledon and the French Open.

44

Pounds of cabbage per person eaten in Russia each year.

- The arts are important in Russia.
- Russia has a long tradition of ballet.
- People celebrate many holidays and festivals throughout the year.

festivals. Christmas is celebrated on January 7, not December 25. This is because the Russian Orthodox religion uses a different calendar.

People in Russia eat a variety of foods. Many Russian dishes contain cabbage, potatoes, or beets. With its long coastline, seafood is also popular. Russians enjoy drinking hot tea.

Golubtsy, or cabbage leaves stuffed with meat and rice, is a favorite Russian dish.

The Health Care System Needs Improvement

Russia's constitution grants all citizens the right to health protection and aid. But health care is not always free. Many patients pay for more or better health care. The Russian Ministry of Health oversees the nation's health care system. Over two million people work in Russia's health care sector.

The medical care people receive in Russia varies widely. Some hospitals in the major cities have the newest high- tech medical equipment. But most Russian medical facilities don't. Patients in rural areas often have to travel far to access health care. Many hospitals have more patients than can be cared for properly.

Russia spends much less of its budget on health care than other nations. The World Health Organization ranked the world's health care systems. Russia's was number 130. This is way below other industrialized countries.

> There's not enough money, medical supplies, and equipment for Russians to get the health care they need.

Russians have access to different medicines like painkillers or antibiotics. But there is also a tradition of home remedies.

Russia has some serious health problems. These include cancer and heart disease. Many Russians do not eat a healthy diet. Obesity affects more than one-quarter of all adults. Pollution in the environment also hurts many Russians' health.

Russians have a lower life expectancy than in most developed nations. In 2017, Russians lived an average of 71 years.

THINK ABOUT IT

In January 2018, the World Bank suggested that Russia increase the amount of money it spends on health care. What areas of medical treatment do you think are important? And how would you spend additional money?

7.1
Percent of Russia's GDP spent on health care.

- The Russian health care system is struggling to meet people's needs
- Russians face a number of serious health problems.
- Russians have a lower life expectancy compared to similar nations.

12

Most Russians Live in Cities

A typical apartment building in Moscow.

609
McDonald's restaurants in Russia in January 2017.

- About three-quarters of Russians live in cities and towns.
- Russian apartments tend to be smaller than those in other countries.
- Russia gets most of its energy from fossil fuels.

People in Russia live in different ways. About three out of four Russians live in cities and towns. Over 12 million people live in Moscow alone. Others live in villages.

Most Russians live in apartments. These apartments are often considered small compared to other countries. The suburbs are filled with huge apartment buildings. Single-family homes are rare.

Wealthier families in Russia's cities often own a second home in the countryside. A country home or summer house is called a dacha. People go to their dachas to enjoy nature and a quieter pace of life.

About one-quarter of Russians live in rural areas. Homes here are often made of wood. Many rural Russians work on collective farms. These were set up during the Soviet era.

Russians in the countryside may also work as miners. But jobs can be hard to come by in rural areas.

About 70 percent of Russia's electricity comes from fossil fuels. These include oil, natural gas, and coal. Russia also uses nuclear energy. This produces radioactive waste. Russia gets about 19 percent of its electricity from waterpower. The country is working to produce more electricity from clean sources, such as solar and wind power.

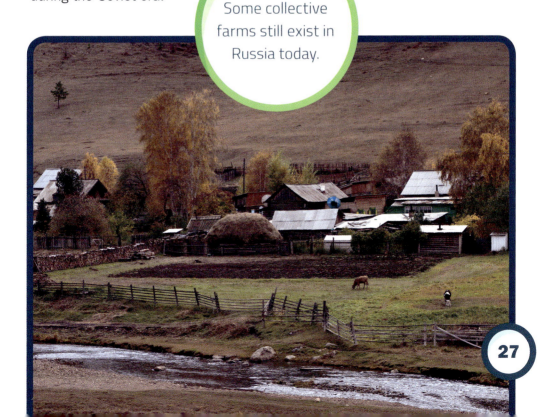

Some collective farms still exist in Russia today.

Russia at a Glance

Population in 2018: 143,971,019

Area: 6,601,668 square miles (17,098,242 sq km)

Capital: Moscow

Largest Cities: Moscow, St. Petersburg, Novosibirsk, Yekaterinburg, Nizhny Novgorod

Flag:

National Language: Russian

Currency: Ruble

What people who live in Russia are called: Russians

Where in the World?

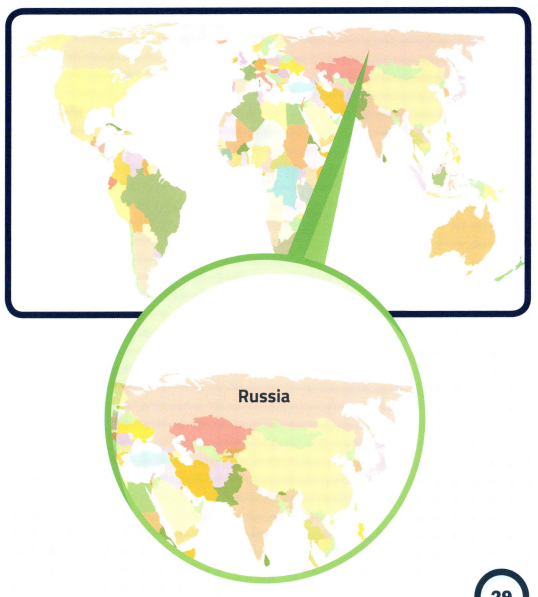

Russia

Glossary

biome
A large ecological community of plants and animals that live in a major habitat.

Cold War
Political hostility between the United States and the USSR from 1945 to 1990.

corruption
Dishonest behavior by the people in power, such as bribery.

cosmonaut
A Russian astronaut.

czar
An emperor of Russia before the 1917 revolution.

democracy
A system of government where citizens elect their leaders.

hydroelectic
The production of electricity by water power.

irrigation
The process of supplying crops or a field with water using artificial means.

nanotechnology
The branch of technology that involves building things on a very tiny scale, such as computer chips.

persecuted
Treated badly because of religion, politics, gender, or some other reason.

steppes
Large areas of unforested, flat grasslands found in southeastern Europe and parts of Asia.

tundra
A large, barren area with no trees and where the ground is usually frozen.

vocational
Involved with the training of a skill or trade to be pursued as a career.

For More Information

Books

Ganeri, Anita. *Journey Through: Russia.* London: Franklin Watts, 2018.

George, Enzo. *Russia's City of the Dead.* Crypts, Tombs, and Secret Rooms. New York: Gareth Stevens Publishing, 2017.

Rechner, Amy. *Russia.* Hopkins, MN: Bellwether Media, 2017.

Regan, Michael. *Vladimir Putin.* Mendota Heights, MN: Focus Readers, 2018.

Visit 12StoryLibrary.com

Scan the code or use your school's login at **12StoryLibrary.com** for recent updates about this topic and a full digital version of this book. Enjoy free access to:

- Digital ebook
- Breaking news updates
- Live content feeds
- Videos, interactive maps, and graphics
- Additional web resources

Note to educators: Visit 12StoryLibrary.com/register to sign up for free premium website access. Enjoy live content plus a full digital version of every 12-Story Library book you own for every student at your school.

Index

About the Author

Alicia Klepeis began her career at the National Geographic Society. She is the author of numerous children's books including *Snakes Are Awesome, Trolls,* and *A Time for Change.* Alicia lives with her family in upstate New York.